GOLD
IN MY
SHOES

Willie Prentice

VICTORY PRESS
LONDON AND EASTBOURNE

© W. Y. Prentice 1971

ISBN 0 85476 131 4

THIS little account of the greatest physical effort of my life is dedicated to Joyce, my dear wife. She did not flinch when I first spoke to her about my 'crazy idea', but gave me her support during the days of preparation, and backed me with her prayers when I was on my journey.

The sound of her cheery voice, when I made my daily phone call, did me a world of good.

'Her children rise up and call her blessed; her husband also, and he praises her.'

Printed in Great Britain for
VICTORY PRESS (Evangelical Publishers Ltd)
Lottbridge Drove, Eastbourne, Sussex
by Errey's Printers, Heathfield.

12
MSC

P06854

Foreword

I HAVE never fancied myself as the author of a book, but so many people have asked me to make the attempt that I have felt constrained to bow to their wishes.

This is the simple story of a sponsored walk I undertook, I believe at the prompting of God, to raise funds for the work of the Hour of Revival Association led by Dr Eric Hutchings.

Some have said that it was the longest sponsored walk ever for the cause of evangelism, but, whether this be true or not, the fact that I, at 66 years of age, managed to walk from Aberdeen to Eastbourne, a distance of nearly 600 miles, should be of interest to some, especially to all my sponsors and hosts.

The success of this walk lay first in the wonderful opportunities I had for personal witness to Christ, and second in the large sum that was raised for Christian work. At the time this book was written, over £3,600 had been received.

In such a long walk there was great variety. The quiet loneliness of Scottish valleys; the soft beauty of the Pentlands Hills; the rugged grandeur of the Pennines; the noise, rush and bustle of Manchester and Birmingham; the classic atmosphere of Oxford; and the thrill of seeing our own Sussex Downs again.

I hope you will enjoy the journey.

EASTBOURNE, 1971   WILLIE PRENTICE

Contents

CHAPTER ONE

How it all began

I was born to Scottish parents in the City of Aberdeen in the year 1905. Owing to my father's indifferent health, he was ordered to the warmer south, and my parents decided to follow this advice, so in the year 1906 they moved to Eastbourne. Other children were born as the years passed and I eventually became the eldest of five, having three brothers and a sister.

When we were old enough we were sometimes taken up to Scotland for our holidays, and we learned to love the Scottish mountains and glens, and I think it was in those days that I developed a love of the open-air. It was a special joy to us to be able to tackle some of Scotland's mountains. We had cousins in Glasgow and they usually joined us in these strenuous excursions. I climbed Ben Lomond three times; ascended Ben Macdhui the second highest mountain in Britain; clambered up Ben More at Crianlarich. Since those days I have 'done' Ben Nevis, Sca Fell, Snowdon, Helvellyn by Striding Edge, and a number of lesser peaks.

As the years went by I never lost the love of walking, and in 1940, with a friend of mine, I walked from the shores of Loch Lomond to Braemar, a distance of 170 miles. This walk which lasted several days took us through the Trossachs, then by Killin, Glen Lyon, Rannoch Moor to Dalnaspidal, and through the Forest of Atholl until we eventually reached Kingussie, Aviemore, and Coylumbridge. One of our main purposes in coming to Scotland was to walk through the Lairig Ghru, a pass through the Cairngorm mountains once much used by cattle drovers. This pass starts at Coylumbridge, climbs to a height of 3000ft. in a distance of seven miles, and then descends very gradually over about 16 miles to the Linn of Dee, which is about five miles from Braemar. We managed to get through this tough day, although a violent thunderstorm forced us to take shelter in Derry Lodge, a substantial building on the lower slopes of Ben Macdhui, which is frequently occupied by deer-stalkers.

It was not surprising, therefore, that when my own family grew up — I have three sons and two daughters — they inherited this same love of walking. The local press once described us as 'The walking Prentices'. On my son Nicolas' 18th birthday in 1962, he and I walked from Tunbridge Wells to Eastbourne, a distance of 30 miles, the last 22 miles being done in pouring rain. When Nicolas was 20, he travelled up to London with two of his friends, and then they walked the whole way back, completing the 63 miles between midnight and 9.30 p.m. the same day. This really set the ball rolling, and soon it was quite normal for my wife and me, or a member of the family, to walk to Brighton from Eastbourne, a distance of 21 miles by the coast road. When I retired in 1965, after 44½ years with Barclays Bank, I walked to Brighton via Lewes, and back to Eastbourne via Seaford, a distance of 45 miles, and I was then 60 years of age.

In more recent years I have explored the Wye Valley from Llangurig to Chepstow, and the South Downs Way from Eastbourne to near Petersfield in Hampshire. In the light of subsequent events, which this little book will relate, I feel sure that in all these experiences God was preparing me for the biggest physical effort of my life. I have thought of the way God prepared David for his great battle with Goliath. David had to tackle the lion and the bear first, but he must have been quite unaware that these experiences were part of God's plan to fit him for the much more difficult task that lay ahead. God has promised to guide His children, but it is often only as we look back over our lives that we are able to see how He has been at work, ordering our circumstances, controlling our impulses, and directing our way. 'He . . . guided them by the skilfulness of his hands' (Psa. 78.72).

CHAPTER TWO

A crazy idea—or was it?

FOR anyone who loves walking, Eastbourne is ideally situated at the foot of the South Downs. These rolling hills give almost unlimited scope for rambles, either of just a few miles or of a score or more. The famous Seven Sisters, lying between Birling Gap and the Cuckmere Valley, provide a walk of exceptional beauty, with a good test for the leg muscles.

It was at the end of October 1970, when I was returning from one of these walks over the downs, that quite suddenly, without warning, or any previous thought of such a thing, the 'Crazy Idea' hit me. I should mention here that since the Hour of Revival Association was formed in 1954 I had been a Board member, and I had enjoyed much fellowship with Dr Eric Hutchings, the dynamic leader of this work, and with the members of his team. In addition to evangelistic crusades, this Association has an extensive radio ministry. For several years the recording studios had been in Terminus Road, Eastbourne, but owing to the expiration of the lease these premises had to be vacated in September 1970. In the goodness of God alternative accommodation was made available at 13 Lismore Road, but much work had to be done and that at considerable expense. All Board members had been asked to share this additional financial burden, and to see what they could do to help. The 'Crazy Idea' that hit me on that last Thursday in October was to do a sponsored walk, and, simultaneously with this thought, Aberdeen came before me. Perhaps it was to be expected that the place of my birth should come up at this time from the sub-conscious. To attempt to walk nearly 600 miles at 65 years of age seemed crazy indeed. However, on returning home I shared my thoughts with my wife and family, and to my surprise they did not tell me I was mad, but at that time they neither encouraged nor discouraged me. I then consulted other trusted friends, including a doctor, and with few exceptions they encouraged me to go ahead with the idea.

Dr Hutchings was busily engaged with a crusade in Cardiff while these things were going on, and it was of course necessary to know what his reactions would be to a sponsored walk to raise funds for his work. I therefore wrote to him in November 1970 and in his reply to my letter he said, "I am thrilled with your letter re the sponsored walk. I think it is a wonderful idea. Go right ahead."

It was about this time, I think, that the Lord Jesus gave me these verses from Judges 18.5, 6 (RSV): 'And they said to him, "Inquire of God, we pray thee, that we may know whether the journey on which we are setting out will succeed." And the priest said to them, "Go in peace. The journey on which you go is under the eye of the Lord."' This was confirmation indeed. The Holy Spirit is the only One who has any right to take a verse of Scripture out of its context and apply it to us and to our circumstances. This He often does, and it is therefore up to us to read our Bibles right through and so give Him plenty of scope. Who would have thought of looking in the Book of Judges for confirmation about a sponsored walk?

In December 1970 I sent out a letter to my many friends and acquaintances, giving them some idea of what I was proposing to do and asking for their support. From the many letters I received in reply, here are a few extracts:

"This is a wonderful idea."

"I think you are crazy."

"It is a tremendous undertaking. Trust you will have a prosperous journey by the will of God."

"I do not think it will be a successful venture viewed from any angle."

"It would be great if you can get sponsors for a total of £1 per mile — then you'll skip along."

"You are a very plucky chap. Wear boots and two pairs of socks to avoid blisters."

"We could fly from Aberdeen to Eastbourne in an hour comfortably." — A friend who flies Tridents.

"Sorry to be so long in replying, but I think it took me several days to get used to the idea of an O.A.P. tramping from Aberdeen to Eastbourne."

"May I wish you every success in your venture, and I am sure the Lord will bless you."

"God speed you. May He keep you fit and alert, and lighten your steps."

"Thy shoes shall be iron and brass; and as thy days, so shall thy strength be."

"Tell Willie Prentice I should like to have been walking with him." — Dr Billy Graham in a letter to Dr Hutchings.

These extracts are a fair sample, and it will be seen that comparatively few were against my doing this walk. I was greatly encouraged.

CHAPTER THREE

Planning and preparation

ONCE I had finally decided to act according to my inner convictions, and the advice and encouragement of my friends, and above all upon the guidance the Lord had given me, there was much to be done. Many things had to be considered. When should I start? It seemed to me that the weeks between Easter and Whitsun 1971 would be about right. The days would not be too hot, and the holiday traffic would not have built up. So I decided to start from Aberdeen on Monday 26th April.

From my experience of walking I felt that I could manage between 20 and 25 miles a day, resting on Sundays. Keeping this in mind, I next turned my attention to my route. It seemed clear that I should use the Tay and Forth road bridges, and this would bring me to South Queensferry, some 15 miles west of Edinburgh. There were several alternatives open to me from this point, but as I wanted to spend a week-end with Rosalyn, my married daughter in Birmingham, I chose my route accordingly. It may surprise some of my readers to be told that Carlisle is due south of Edinburgh, and I therefore decided to cross the border near Canonbie, and to proceed via Carlisle to the south. With the help of Ordnance Survey maps, borrowed from the local library, I studied my route in more detail, and after much consideration I was able to fix on 27 stopping places, with distances of 20 to 28 miles between them.

My next concern was to get my accommodation fixed up at each stopping place, as it can be very frustrating to arrive in an unfamiliar town or village after a long and tiring day on the road, and have to start looking for somewhere to spend the night. As the postal strike was on at the time, my task was not an easy one, but I was able to make quite a few arrangements by telephone. Fortunately I have relations in the Edinburgh area, and also at Birmingham and Camberley in Surrey; I also have friends in Blackburn and Oxford, and Haywards Heath in Sussex. Dr Eric Hutchings with his wide circle of supporters was able to locate those 'given to hospitality' whose homes were on or near my route. So, by the end of March, with one or two exceptions this part of my planning was completed. As things eventually turned out, I stayed at eight hotels; six nights I was with relations, and thirteen nights with friends.

At the beginning of December 1970 I began a series of weekly preparation walks varying in distance from 20 to 30 miles, and these continued until mid-April when I walked on three consecutive days covering 63 miles. As most of my Sponsored Walk was to be on the roads, and I should be carrying a rucksack with all my requirements, I did a lot of my preparation walks on the roads also carrying a loaded rucksack. Between the beginning of December and the middle of April I walked over 500 miles; this paid off, as during the 'big walk' I had no cramp or serious stiffness. I also practised a little self-control in the matter of eating and was able to get my weight down by a few pounds. In addition to all this I made it my practice to swab my feet daily with surgical spirit for several weeks before starting out on my big task.

And so the time drew near for my adventure. Final decisions had to be made about the contents of my rucksack. The weather can be cold in Scotland in April and May, so I had to include some warm clothing; I also needed suitable attire for the evenings and Sundays. My aunt in Aberdeen, with whom I spent my first week-end, was quite relieved when I turned up for breakfast on Sunday morning with long trousers, a nylon shirt and tie, and a nice blue anorak. She was afraid I would be making my way to church in shorts. I did in fact do all my walking in shorts, a T-shirt and a roll-neck pullover. When it was cold I wore an anorak, and I also had with me a Cagoule for protection against rain. This is a splendid garment, made of nylon, very light, with a zip up to the chin, and of mid-thigh length, so that in rain most of me would be kept dry. In addition to this I packed my things in polythene bags in my rucksack. My only other piece of equipment was a stout walking-stick which I bought in Llangurig, when I did my walk through the Wye valley. I have carried this with me on all my walks since then and it must have been with me over more than 1500 miles. I decided not to take a camera or my electric shaver as these would have added unnecessary weight to my rucksack, which I managed to get down to about 16lb.

On Friday 23rd April a small group of friends met in our home and joined in prayer for me, that God's blessing might rest on every step of my way. Someone prayed 'that every place that the soles of your feet shall tread upon might be claimed for God.' This prayer had a special significance, as I was to learn a few days later.

I had booked a seat on the 'Flying Scotsman', one of British Rail's crack trains, which leaves Kings Cross at 10 a.m. This meant an early start for me on Saturday morning 24th April, and I had to catch the 6.37 train from Eastbourne. When I got to Kings Cross I had time to spare, so I went into the buffet there and had a cup of coffee and a ham sandwich, and as I enjoyed these I extracted my New Testament and Psalms from my rucksack and read some verses about walking, in the Epistle to the Ephesians. My spirit thrilled as I read, '. . . trespasses and sins, in which *you once walked* . . .' (Chap. 2. 1, 2 RSV). I praised God for that past tense which so forcibly reminded me of God's delivering grace.

What a train the 'Flying Scotsman' is! London to Edinburgh—400 miles in $5\frac{3}{4}$ hours, with one stop at Newcastle. I timed the speed of this train at one point and found that we were travelling at 110 m.p.h. Perhaps one of the worst parts of my 'adventure' was sitting in this fast and comfortable train as it rushed northwards, and thinking that I should be attempting to *walk* back all those miles. Perhaps I *was* 'bonkers', after all. These reflections did not put me off my food, and I enjoyed my B.R. lunch of mushroom soup, steak and kidney pie, and fruit salad. As I ate we were passing through flat agricultural country where there were huge fields of pale green, where shoots of winter wheat, oats and barley, encouraged by the recent rains, gave evidence of the harvest to come. I thought . . . no sowing; no harvest. I praised God for the sowing of the good seed of the Word of God in my life at a very early age, and for all those who had tended the new life. One of my earliest recollections of spiritual things was sitting on my grandmother's knee in Aberdeen and learning verses of scripture. Oddly enough, I can still remember several of these verses, although I could not have been more than four or five. One is 'I love them that love me; and those that seek me early shall find me' (Prov. 8. 17); and another from Revelation 22. 12, 'Behold, I come quickly; and my reward is with me, to give every man according as his work shall be.'

We drew into Waverley Station, Edinburgh dead on time, and I had to change trains here; I still had about 130 miles to go. The final part of my journey had the added attraction of the crossing of the Forth and Tay bridges. The day had been cloudy and dull with no sight of the sun, but as we moved on to the Tay bridge the sun burst forth in all its glory, and everything looked quite different. I was reminded of that most wonderful of all bridges, built at infinite cost by our Lord Jesus, from earth to heaven. Whoever crosses that bridge will find that the Sun of Righteousness will arise with healing in His wings, and all things will look quite different. We shall see the glory of God in the face of Jesus Christ. With these meditations still fresh in my mind we pulled into Aberdeen at 7.40 p.m.; I had been 13 hours on the journey from Eastbourne.

CHAPTER FOUR

Count-down and take-off

ALTHOUGH most of my relations in Aberdeen have died,
I still have a very active and hospitable aunt who opened
her home to me for my final week-end before 'taking off'.

I was very surprised to see the trees and flowers so far
advanced, but I learned that the winter had been un-
usually mild, and there had been little frost and no snow
—a thing almost unheard of in Aberdeen. Oddly enough,
when I started my Walk on the Monday morning it was
snowing in Eastbourne, but—no sign of snow in Aberdeen.

This brief stay in the place where I was born proved
to be a really happy time. On Sunday morning I went
with Mrs. Henzel Salter, my aunt, to the Brethren Assembly at Hebron Hall, and sought to worship the Lord and
remember Him in the 'breaking of bread', with a good
company of the saints. I think this was the first time I had
ever been in a Brethren morning meeting when a dog was
present. This turned out to be Dusty, a lovely Labrador
owned by Miss Meryl Sanderson who was born blind, and
who lives in her flat with only the dog for company. A
cousin of mine and his wife, who invited me for lunch
and tea, also made it their practice to have Meryl with
them for these meals on Sundays, and it was in their home
that I learned something about guide dogs for the blind
which I did not know before. My relations had a West
Highland terrier, and it was great fun to watch Dusty,
the big Labrador, chasing the little terrier all round the
lounge. It was difficult to understand how Dusty, with all
this boundless energy, could be of any use to a blind person. And then Meryl told me the secret. As soon as she
placed the harness on her dog, his behaviour changed;
he became obedient and entirely dependable. The high
spirits were still there, but with the harness on he was
under his owner's authority. I thought of those verses,
'Take my yoke upon you and learn of me', and 'Put ye

on the Lord Jesus Christ.' What a wonderful lesson I learned that day! What a joy it is to take His yoke and put ourselves under His authority! We can be of real use to Him, and He can harness our high spirits, direct our impulses, guide our desires, control our tempers, and give to us His peace.

After the evening service at Hebron Hall, about 100 young people gathered for their informal sing-song and I had the privilege of speaking about my Sponsored Walk for a few minutes. And so the day ended with my retiring for the night into the first of the 27 beds. I would be sleeping in during my journey south.

Monday 26th April was dry but there was a cold wind blowing from the north east. My aunt, whose hospitality I have already mentioned, provided me with an ample and excellent breakfast. I had risen quite early, and had my usual cold bath and Quiet Time with the Lord, and I really enjoyed the food set before me, and I was 'raring' to go.

I have always found it a good practice to start my walks at about 9 a.m., walk for $3\frac{1}{2}$ to 4 hours, then have a picnic lunch, and rest for an hour or so, before setting off on the final stages. On this my first morning I was somewhat delayed by the visit of several representatives of the Aberdeen Press, who wanted to check my story and get some photographs. They called at the house at 8.50 and got what they come for, and then asked me to go with them to the Bridge of Dee on the outskirts of Aberdeen, for a final picture. I have to admit that although the air was cold I was shivering a bit for other reasons. Here I was, nearly 600 miles from home, and about to try to walk all that way back at nearly 66 years of age. Six months had passed since the idea of doing this Walk had first come to me. The Lord had encouraged me, I believe, from His Word, and many of my friends had promised to pray for me, and the sponsoring figure had grown far beyond my expectations. As I stood there on that cold April morning, I knew that I would be earning about £5 for every mile I walked. With all my preparation and training I felt in tip-top physical condition, but perhaps I shivered a little as I thought of the heavy responsibility resting upon me. However this weakness soon passed as I waved farewell to my friends and set out on the road to Stonehaven.

When planning my route I had seriously considered taking the Deeside road from Aberdeen, and going via Ballater, Braemar, over the Devil's Elbow, and on to Perth. This would have added quite a few miles to my itinerary, with some pretty stiff climbing on the way. At the Bridge of Dee I saw the Ballater road right before me, and I had some regrets that I was not going to walk through some of the loviest scenery in Scotland. But I felt that I had made the right decision and so it was towards Stonehaven I went.

CHAPTER FIVE

Getting into my stride

MOST of my walking had to be done on main roads, and I always made it my practice to walk on the right, facing the traffic, unless there was a footpath in which case I used it. Before leaving Eastbourne I had taken out a Personal Accident Policy for £5000 with Lloyds of London, at a very reasonable premium. This covered me against the loss of life, eye or limb, but in the goodness of God I did not have to make any claim, in spite of the many real dangers when the traffic was heavy and drivers were sometimes a bit reckless. Hebrews 1. 14 tells us of the angels, who are ministering spirits sent forth to serve those who are to obtain salvation. I like to feel that I was favoured with this angelic protection, perhaps as a result of the many prayers which were made on my behalf.

Soon after leaving Aberdeen I saw a man repairing some telephone wires, and I spoke to him and discovered that he had booked in for a conference in Eastbourne in September in connection with the Ancient Order of Shepherds of which he was a member. A little later that morning I was discovered by a man in a car who turned out to be a photographer from the Aberdeen Press. He wanted to see how I was getting on and get a picture for his paper. The Aberdeen Press gave me good coverage and phoned through to my wife in Eastbourne several times to get up-to-date news of my progress. They seemed to have some insight into one of the main purposes of my Walk when they used the phrase, 'Hitting the hallelujah trail'.

The rest of that day passed without incident and I was glad when I reached Gourdon, a picturesque fishing village down by the sea, some 24 miles from Aberdeen. The Commercial Hotel provided me with all I needed—a good hot bath, an excellent meal, and a comfortable bed. I turned in at 8 p.m.

I left Gourdon the following morning at 9 and I was
glad to be able to walk by a cliff path for about six miles,
and then by the disused railway track as far as Montrose.
This is a busy little town with a wide main street and a
good shopping centre. I bought some soft rolls, fruit and
a yoghurt for my lunch. I always carried some butter and
jam in Tupperware containers to go with the rolls. If the
weather was fine I looked out for a suitable place to have
my lunch; this was usually a park or field. And after my
snack I liked to get my head on my rucksack and have
an hour or so resting. If I could put in $3\frac{1}{2}$ to 4 hours
walking and cover 12 to 14 miles before this break, I was
well pleased. I also had a vacuum flask with me, and this
was filled with coffee or tomato soup, or sometimes orange
juice. Drink can be quite a problem on a long walk, as
liquid is heavy and one does need plenty. It was of course
possible to refill my flask from time to time. These mid-
day lunch breaks became quite important to me and I
looked forward to taking my rucksack off and resting for
a while. Quite often as it drew near to 12.30 I would say
to the Lord, "Lord, you were very good at finding suitable
resting places for the children of Israel when they jour-
neyed through the wilderness; I should appreciate it if you
would direct me to a good place for my lunch." I believe
He often answered this simple prayer. It is wonderful to
be able to talk to the Lord like this. He is far above all
principality and power; His Name is above every name;
He is seated at the right hand of God. He is the centre
of heaven's worship, yet we who have received Him as
our Saviour may be on intimate terms with Him and talk
to Him about everything.

I left Montrose, crossed the bridge over the river Esk,
took the Lunan road and got to Arbroath at 6 p.m. I had
covered nearly 50 miles in the first two days. I stayed for
the night at The Elms, a home for the children of mis-
sionaries, run at the present time by Mr. & Mrs. Potter.
Owing to the unexpected arrival of some parents, I had
to share a room and sleep in the lower of two bunk beds,
quite a novel experience for me.

CHAPTER SIX

My poor feet

MY feet were causing me some concern as they had become blistered and painful. This greatly surprised me, for
I had done so many miles in my preparation walks, and
I had regularly used surgical spirit, and tested out the
shoes I was to wear. I believe that my foot trouble had
more than a physical explanation. I recalled that prayer
in our home when someone prayed for the soles of my
feet, and it seemed that the devil was allowed to attack
me just there. This could also have been one of the Lord's
ways of keeping me humble, and dependent on Him. I
was directed to Psalm 39. 4, '... that I may know how
frail I am.'

In spite of the condition of my feet I managed to get
started at 9 a.m., and left Arbroath by the main Dundee
road. The special interest of this day was to be the crossing of the Tay Bridge, which links Dundee with Newport-
on-Tay. Before getting there I had to cover about 20
miles. At about mid-day I began to think of getting some
food, and in the goodness of God I spotted a small café.
I had just spoken to a man standing in a field of rasp-
berry canes, and he informed me that there were 80 acres
of them, owned by Smedleys. He felt that there was over-
production in this sphere, and they had real problems
getting a sufficient labour force to pick the fruit when
ripe.

The café appeared to be run by a buxom, good-natured
woman assisted by her two daughters, one of whom was
married and had a little girl running around. The buxom
woman told me that she had walked from John O'Groats
to Lands End with a party organised by Sir Billy Butlin.
I had a first-rate meal, all for 25p, relaxed in a comfortable chair, and then went on my way refreshed by good
food and good company.

Much to my surprise I reached the sign reading 'City of

Dundee' at 2 p.m., but it took me $2\frac{1}{2}$ hours to get to the Tay Bridge from there. This bridge is nearly $1\frac{1}{2}$ miles long, and it took me nearly half an hour to cross. What a contrast there is between Dundee lying on the north bank of the River Tay and Newport on the south bank. Dundee with its population of 182,000, Scotland's third largest city—just slightly ahead of Aberdeen—and Newport a small town of only 3300 or so. As I came off the bridge I spotted an A.A. scout who directed me to the Seymour Hotel where I was to stay for the night. They did not appear to be very busy and were therefore able to give me every attention. I had been allocated bedroom No. 1 with bathroom attached, and I was able to luxuriate in a hot bath prior to my evening meal. Before turning in at 8.30 I read Psalm 37 and was particularly impressed with verse 23, 'The steps of a good man are ordered by the Lord; and he delighteth in his way.'

I got up at 7 a.m.—it was my 66th birthday—and I praised the Lord for His wonderful goodness to me through all the years.

My feet were really in poor shape and the heel of one of my shoes was badly in need of attention. I was directed to a Mr. Blicharski who had a shoe repairing business at the far end of the town. Before calling on him I felt it necessary to buy a bottle of codeine tablets, because the pain in my feet was making it increasingly difficult to keep going, and I was determined to get to Edinburgh at all costs because I would be staying with relations there. As I entered Mr. Blicharski's shop I said to him, "I can see that you have skilled hands; I hope you have a kind heart, because I have an emergency job for you." While he examined my shoes I said, "I am quite sure you can mend my shoes, but I am equally sure that you cannot do anything for my feet." He said, pointing to my shoes, "You will always have trouble with your feet if you go on wearing these rubber-soled shoes." I had worn these same shoes frequently on my preparation walks at home, and I was greatly puzzled by what he said. I know of course that it is generally felt that leather-soled boots or shoes are correct for long distance walking, but a fortnight before

leaving Eastbourne I had walked 63 miles in three consecutive days in my rubber-soled shoes with no ill effects.
What should 1 do? Ignore the advice of my Polish friend
or buy another pair of shoes? I chose the latter course,
and purchased a pair of leather-soled Grenson Ortho-
paedics for £7.50. The new shoes seemed comfortable and,
after walking about 10 miles to Cupar, Fife, I posted my
others home.

CHAPTER SEVEN

Breaking the 'sound barrier'

MANY Christians will readily admit that when it comes to personal witnessing they are rather like the St. Lawrence River in winter—frozen at the mouth. When the opportunity is given and we feel we should speak to someone about Christ, there is a barrier, and we find it difficult to break through. I must say that I have often found this to be the case, but on my long walk I seemed to be free from fear and restraint and I rejoiced in the liberty given to me to speak to folk about my Lord. During my first week, when I was suffering so much with my feet, the Lord gave me some of my best opportunities of witnessing for Him. In His own tender and loving way He balances up our experiences, so that what we may count as loss can prove to be gain.

Some 20 miles from Newport-on-Tay I approached the small town of Windygates. My feet were painful and I was feeling tired, and as I walked down the main street I saw a man of middle age coming towards me and I asked him to direct me to the Windygates Inn where I was to stay for the night. He did this and then said, "You are Willie Prentice, aren't you? I am just going to our church prayer meeting, and we are going to pray for you." I had never been in Windygates in my life, and how thrilling to know that there was a group of Christians here who were praying for me! If this were true in this place, how many other groups were also 'helping me by prayer'?

The Windygates Inn was at the bottom of the hill, and I entered the bar by the swing doors. Several men were there having a drink, and one of them said to me, "Where have you come from?" I said, "I left Newport this morning." Then, looking at my rucksack which I had put down, he said, "What, carrying that thing?" I said, "Yes." Then he came over, picked up my rucksack and said, "Jesus Christ!" I looked straight at him and said, "How wonderful that you should say that! The Lord Jesus Christ is the One I am walking for. He is my Lord, and my Saviour. He is a very wonderful person." The man looked puzzled; he had probably never connected his blasphemous utterance with the Son of God.

Later that evening I was told that the 'boys' wanted me to go down to the bar as they wanted to celebrate my 66th birthday. Owing to an incorrect Press report, there had been some confusion in Windygates about me. The Press had put it out that I was born in Windygates, whereas in fact I was born in Aberdeen. Some of the 'gaffers' who were born around 1905 and had lived in Windygates all their lives could not recall anyone named Willie Prentice, and I believe some of them had even searched some of the parish records without success. However, the 'boys' knew it was my 66th, and I felt it right to accept their invitation; so about 9 p.m. I strolled into the bar. (What would you have done?) They asked me, "What will you have? A whisky?" I explained that I was really a non-drinker, but I was touched by their kindness and I asked for a small cider. As I sipped my drink I had the unusual privilege of talking to a man about the Lord Jesus, sitting in the bar of a 'pub'.

Although I had cut down the contents of my rucksack to a minimum, I felt it wise to take a supply of gospel booklets with me. I chose, 'Becoming a Christian' by the Rev. J. R. W. Stott, and in the front I wrote my name and address, and mentioned '. . . on a sponsored walk from Aberdeen to Eastbourne'. I started out with 20 and was able to pick up another 20 in Edinburgh. These were all used during my Walk, following personal conversations.

I was particularly pleased to have numerous opportunities of witnessing to the Press and the B.B.C. Representatives of these sometimes called to see me at my temporary home, or they found me on the road. Press handouts had been sent to about 100 different newspapers and the editors had been furnished with the names and addresses of my hotels and hosts, so they knew where to find me.

The inn at Windygates was a bit rough and ready as it had recently been taken over by new proprietors, and the previous owners had left things rather below standard; but the food was good and I was shown every kindness. I spent my usual 20 minutes or so changing the Elastoplast on my blisters, took my codeine tablets and set off about 9 a.m. The day was misty but fine and I was looking forward to crossing the Forth Bridge at the end of my day. Arrangements had been made for me to stay with a cousin of mine who lives in Falkirk. He had kindly offered to pick me up at South Queensferry at the southern end of the bridge, take me to his home in Falkirk for the night and return me to South Queensferry the following morning. He was in the insurance business and worked in Kirkcaldy, and, as I had to pass through this delightful town in the morning, we had arranged to meet for coffee. This made a pleasant break for me, for it can be a bit lonely walking all day by oneself. My cousin offered to take my rucksack, which was a great help. I carried a small knapsack with me, in which I could put my lunch and my Cagoule in case of rain, and I used this when I was able to get 'transport' for my rucksack. The road from Kirkcaldy took me by the Firth of Forth, and at my lunch time I discovered a delightful spot overlooking the Forth where I was able to eat and sunbathe. The approach to the mighty bridge is awe-inspiring, and is in keeping with this massive constructon. Like the Tay Bridge it is about $1\frac{1}{2}$ miles long. My cousin, who is the son of my aunt in Aberdeen with whom I stayed, picked me up at South Queensferry, as arranged, and took me to his home in Falkirk, a distance of about 18 miles.

That evening I was given the opportunity of speaking to a lively group of teens and twenties who meet on Friday evenings in connection with the Brethren Assembly. I was asked to speak briefly about my Walk and then to take a short epilogue. I mounted the platform wearing a pair of very light travelling slippers, and my cousin in introducing me spoke about my Walk as 'no mean feat'. This caused some amusement. Before I left, I was handed two gifts of £5 and £2 for the work of the Hour of Revival. We turned in at 11 p.m.

My first week was drawing to an end, and as I was set down at South Queensferry I bade farewell to my cousin and his wife, and set off once again. My original plan had been to reach Peebles, but with my blistered and bruised feet I realised I would never get that far—about 30 miles. Without my codeine tablets I would not have been able to walk at all, but with the aid of the pain-killers I managed to get going. My route lay through the small town of Currie, and from there I planned to take a footpath through the Pentland Hills to Penicuik (pronounced Penicook). Near the centre of Currie I spotted a group of lads and I asked them to confirm that I was on the right road for the Harlaw Farm where the footpath began. They said I was on the right road, and then I said, "How important it is to be on the right road." I told them a little bit about what I was doing, and one of the lads went away and fetched several others; the group of 8 or 9 seemed interested, so I said, "I can tell you the right road to heaven in a sentence. Jesus said, 'I am the way, the truth, and the life: no man cometh unto the Father, but by me, (John 14. 6)." I handed out several of my booklets and continued on my way. I felt grateful to God for this opportunity of speaking to these fellows who possessed such tremendous potential.

I found the footpath without much trouble and crossed the gentle Pentland Hills by the Threipmuir reservoir. When I felt I must be getting near to Penicuik I asked a man how far it was. He said it was about nine miles, and my heart sank. I should say here that I did not carry any maps with me, but I had made brief notes of information taken from the Ordnance Survey maps I had studied before leaving Eastbourne. I was therefore sometimes dependent on information I could obtain from others on the road. This information was frequently miles away from the truth, as in this case. Penicuik was in fact only $2\frac{1}{2}$ miles away. As I entered this place I met three folk to whom I spoke, and they turned out to be Christians who promised to pray for me at their Church prayer meeting.

CHAPTER EIGHT

Resting in the capital

FROM a phone box I called my relations in Edinburgh with whom I was to stay, and they came out by car and fetched me back to their lovely home. The household consists of Mum and Dad, Henzel and John Brunton—Henzel is the daughter of my Aberdeen aunt—and their four daughters: Audrey age 10; Eunice 8; and Margaret and Grace, five-year-old twins. This home proved to a Palace Beautiful to me. I was so glad to have got through to my first Saturday with the prospect of a good rest on Sunday, and the chance to get some attention to my feet. In the church where my folk go there is a chiropodist, Mr. Bachop, and he very kindly agreed to see me on Sunday afternoon. After he had examined my feet he asked me what my plans were. I told him that I had hoped to continue on my journey the following day, but he said this was out of the question, and asked me to see him again on the following Wednesday. I was now faced with two alternatives: (1) Call the walk off, (2) Rest for a few days and then continue.

Apart from my feet I was feeling extremely well, and to give up was unthinkable. I decided therefore to lay up for a week and continue exactly seven days late. This was annoying as I would have to advise all my hotels and hosts of this delay and give them the opportunity to contact me in case they could not put me up. I did this by telephone and letter, and with one exception they could manage the new dates.

Quite contrary to my normal routine, I stayed in bed on the Sunday morning until 10 o'clock and then had breakfast. While the others went off to the Family Service I rested in a deck-chair in the garden in lovely sunshine. This fine weather continued for several days, and I soaked up as much sun as possible. On Monday and Tuesday the four girls were around as they had holidays because of the local elections, and the school premises were being used as polling stations. I ought to have mentioned Darkie the Aberdeen terrier who was a much-loved member of the Brunton household.

By Tuesday I thought I could detect a slight improvement in the condition of my feet and I was looking forward to my visit to Mr. Bachop. When he examined me on Wednesday evening he said, "I would not have believed that so much improvement could have taken place in such a short time." I knew that many folk were praying about my feet, especially in Eastbourne, and God had surely heard their prayers. With fresh bandages on I felt encouraged and confident, and in my reading that evening I was impressed with part of Romans 8. 28—'. . . called according to his purpose.' All along I had felt that I had been called to do this Walk, and that it was God's plan for me, and I could not see it being abandoned. Two more days' rest would bring me to Saturday, when I hoped to be able to complete my unfinished walk from Penicuick to Peebles, and thus be ready to start from there on Monday May 10th, a week later than originally planned.

On Thursday morning, wearing my travelling slippers, I managed to cut the lawn, and in the afternoon I walked a short distance to the post office, and then took Darkie for a short scamper in the nearby park. My cousin, Henzel, had to take Darkie into the city to be stripped on Friday morning, so I joined them in the car, and was dropped off near Princes Street. I managed to walk the length of this beautiful road, with its elegant shops on one side and hanging gardens on the other, the Castle high up on the rock. It was a fine morning and everything was looking its best. I bought several pairs of woollen socks in Princes Street, and then replenished my stock of booklets at McCall Barbour's shop on George IV Bridge. I must have walked about $2\frac{1}{2}$ miles before catching a bus to Liberton Drive, where I was staying. In my reading that morning I came across Romans 10.15, 'How beautiful are the feet of them that . . . bring glad tidings of good things!" I prayed, "O God, make this abundantly true in my case."

I woke to the sound of rain on the Saturday morning, and I was a little concerned as this was the day in which I was going to test out my feet by walking from Penicuik to Peebles, a distance of about 14 miles. By 8 a.m. the rain had eased off and John Brunton took me in his car to Penicuik, and I was able to get off at 9.15. I felt well and strode off at my usual pace, minus my rucksack, because I would be returning to Edinburgh for the week-end. I did the 14 miles in 4 hours, average $3\frac{1}{2}$ miles per hour, and my feet stood up to this test very well. It had been arranged for the Bruntons to come out to Peebles, bringing a picnic lunch with them, and join me there. We found a delightful spot down by the River Tweed, and enjoyed an ample meal provided by Mrs. Brunton.

After a short rest—much to the annoyance of the four girls—we set off in the car and John took us through magnificent scenery, returning to Edinburgh via Selkirk. We had done about 80 miles, and reached 'home' at 7.30 p.m.

To-morrow, Sunday, would be my last rest day in Edinburgh, as on Monday I had to get back to the real purpose of my visit to Scotland. It would be quite strange taking to the road again, and becoming detached.

My second Sunday in Scotland's capital was a very happy one. My feet were still improving after the 14 mile test of the previous day. Before breakfast I read, 'Let us walk honestly, as in the day' (Rom. 13. 13). My host asked me if I would lead some choruses at the evening service, and I readily agreed as I had so much enjoyed singing 'spiritual songs' while I plodded along the roads.

And so this unexpected interlude in Edinburgh came to an end. I was treated like a V.I.P. by my relations; Mr. Bachop, the chiropodist, had been used to get me walking again; I had enjoyed a real rest and felt ready to re-commence my Walk. There must have been some definite purpose in the week's delay. After my return to Eastbourne I received a letter from one of my sponsors, in which I read, "Well done I kept to your schedule in prayer, but the Holy Spirit would have adjusted the requests in His timetable."

CHAPTER NINE

Farewell, Scotland

As John Brunton had to be at his work by 8.45 a.m., and he had kindly offered to take me to Peebles, it was necessary to make an early start. I overslept, but got up at 6.30 and had breakfast with the family; then John and I set off for Peebles at 7.15. We got there at 7.50 so I had a nice early start. I was wearing a very light pair of suede leather shoes given to me by Milward & Sons Ltd., who had also sponsored me. These I found to be most comfortable, and I wore them for a good many of the remaining miles. I was also given a very good pair of shoes by Victor Down Ltd. of Eastbourne. They were oiled leather with leather soles, and had commando type rubber soles on top of the leather ones. Unfortunately I did not have sufficient time to break these in before leaving my home town, but I was able to make good use of them from time to time.

I took the Traquair road from Peebles, and soon found myself in delightful country. As this was a 'B' road the traffic was light, and as I went on I had the road more and more to myself. The scenery was superb, with strenuous ascents through two beautiful valleys. This is a sheep rearing area and I must have seen many thousands of sheep with their lambs. Many of the lambs looked 'bloody' for they had recently had their tails cut. In June all the sheep are gathered in and sorted out according to their markings. The lambs had no markings as this is not necessary, for at 'gathering time' they stay close by their mothers, and there is never any difficulty in determining to which farmer they belong.

Because of my early start I reached my destination for the day at 5 p.m.. This was the Tushielaw Inn at Ettrick Water, quite remote, but popular with those who are keen on fishing. I had made it my custom to phone through to my wife in Eastbourne as soon as I had completed my

walk for the day, unless this happened to be before 6 p.m.,
in which case I waited until the cheap rate came into
operation; was this because of my Aberdonian origin?
These brief contacts with my home were full of interest
as we exchanged our news. I had fixed a large map of
Britain on one of the doors of our living-room and in-
dicated my route and stopping places on it. I had also
stuck up a list of my hotels and hosts together with their
adddresses and telephone numbers. My daughter Caroline
made it her job each day to draw a thick blue line down
the map, showing where I had got to in my 'pilgrimage'.
When I phoned from the Tushielaw Inn I learned that
someone had sponsored me for 20p per mile, which re-
presented £114 for the 570 miles I hoped to complete. I
also heard that many people had been praying for me,
especially about my 'feet trouble'. My readers will no
doubt be glad to know that after the seven hours' walking
of this day my feet were feeling fine, and I do not think
I need refer to them again. That evening the Lord gave
me Psalm 34.6, 'This poor man cried, and the Lord heard
him, and saved him out of all his troubles.'

At the evening meal I met three other guests; I believe
they were the only ones besides myself. They were
charming in manner and appearance, were of the retired
colonel type and were there on a fishing holiday. They
seemed interested in my Walk, which the proprietor had
told them about, and one of them kindly offered to take
my rucksack to Langholm the next day. May the Lord
bless him for this kindness. I turned in early and had
10 hours in bed.

The Tushielaw Inn is run by a man and his wife, as in
this isolated spot it is almost impossible to obtain staff.
Because of this I could not have my breakfast before
9 a.m. and this meant that I was unable to get started on
my Walk before about 9.45. It was fine again, with bright
sunshine and the prospect of a good day. It was also
May 11th, a special anniversary for my wife and me,
because it was on this date in 1941 that our bungalow
was demolished by an enemy bomb, just six months after
our wedding. As the house came crashing down about us,

the words from Psalm 91 came into my mind: 'He shall cover thee with his feathers.' It has been our habit to praise the Lord on this date each year for His protection and care on that early Sunday morning in 1941.

Without my rucksack I felt really light-hearted as I took to the road for Langholm. Soon after leaving the inn I spotted a small shop calling itself 'The Ettrick Stores', so I decided to go in and buy a few things for my midday snack. It was as well I did, because this shop turned out to be the only one between Peebles and Langholm, a distance of about 48 miles which I covered in two days. This part of the border country is very thinly populated, has no railways, and buses are few and far between. I was glad it was fine as I walked through the Eskdalemuir area, for this is reputed to be the wettest place in Britain. Some years ago over 4 inches of rain fell there in a few hours, and several road bridges were carried away. In the late afternoon a light drizzle began to fall, but not enough to cause me any discomfort. As I pursued my solitary way, a car coming towards me stopped, and a man got out and introduced himself as a Mr. Espley who used to live in Eastbourne and was a member of the Upperton Congregational Church. He had recognised me, although he did not know I was on a sponsored walk; it was good to stop and have a chat with him.

I didn't get to my hotel in Langholm until 7.40; this was exceptionally late for me, but was partly due to my late start from the Tushielaw Inn, and to the fact that I had to cover nearly 30 miles. The Eskdale Hotel made me very comfortable. This was to be my last 'home' in Scotland. My host in Carlisle was to have been Pastor Frost of the Pentecostal Church, but owing to my week's delay he could not have me, as he was away at a conference. I therefore phoned through to the Press in Carlisle, with whom I had already had contact. They recommended a suitable hotel, so I booked a room.

My last day in Scotland was full of interest. After about $2\frac{1}{2}$ hours' walking I reached the delightful village of Canonbie which is about 3 miles from the border

between Scotland and England. Representatives of the
B.B.C. and the Press were waiting for me. They had come
out from Carlisle to check up on my 'story' and get some
pictures. Some film was also taken, which, I was informed,
would be used at 5.50 that evening on Border News and
T.V. I must say that I always found the Press and B.B.C.
representatives courteous and helpful; one of them in Sussex even bought me a choc-ice. Knowing that my 'friends'
had come out from Carlisle, I asked them to take my
rucksack to my hotel there. I also had a spare pair of
shoes which badly needed repairing, and they took these
to a shoe repairer in Carlisle and left the address at the
hotel.

After this pleasant delay I got going again, and was
glad to have the lovely River Esk for company; and when
the time came for my lunch break I found a delightful
spot where I was able to have a swim, before eating and
resting.

The time to say farewell to Scotland was near as I
walked towards Scots Dyke. It was quite a thrill to see
the signpost marked, 'Cumberland'. I had been walking in
Dumfriesshire for a good many miles, and since leaving
Aberdeen I had trudged through 8 counties altogether.
By the time I reached Eastbourne I would have walked
through 19 different counties. At Scots Dyke I had
walked about 200 miles; I was a third of the way home.

CHAPTER TEN

Another set-back

CARLISLE is a busy town with a population of over 70,000, and my hotel was right in the centre, near the railway station. As I passed through the main shopping area, a man selling newspapers must have recognised me for he called out and pointed to the front page of the paper he was selling, and there was I in the picture taken earlier that day at Canonbie. There was also a short article about my Walk. I was given a complimentary copy.

My hotel had an impressive look about it — the entrance lounge with its red carpet; the attractive girl in the reception desk; the head porter in his smart uniform; and a quiet air of prosperity. After my bath and an evening meal, I did something which I should not have done in a decent hotel — I washed some of my things in the wash-basin in my bedroom. I always carried a small quantity of Persil or Tide with me. This was an easy job, but the problem was to get the things dry. I sought out the porter and asked to be conducted to a drying-room, or similar place. After getting permission from the manager he took me 'behind the scenes' to the boiler-room. As soon as we got away from the attractive public part of the hotel, we came upon dust, dirt and dilapidation. What a contrast! My mind turned at once to those words in Psalm 51, 'Thou desirest truth in the inward being; therefore teach me wisdom in my secret heart' (RSV). And also I Samuel 16.7, 'For the Lord sees not as man sees; man looks on the outward appearance, but the Lord looks on the heart' (RSV). It is good to have an attractive exterior, but God is far more concerned with what we are 'underneath'. By His Holy Spirit, and on the ground of the precious blood that was shed for us upon the cross, God is able to deal effectively with the unseen things in our lives which rob us of our

joy, spoil our witness, and steal away our spiritual power
. . . such were some of my reflections as I turned in for
the night.

This proved to be the noisiest night I spent while on
my walk. The hotel was near a large building site, where
a top priority job appeared to be in progress day and
night. All through the night lorries continued to unload
bricks or hardcore, men were singing, and a real hulla-
baloo was going on. Sleep was well-nigh impossible.

Strangely enough my second set-back occurred that
night — I had an attack of diarrhoea. I must have picked
up a germ somewhere. In the morning my mouth was
dry, and I could not face food.

I left the hotel at 8.45, collected my shoes which had
been repaired, and made my way out of Carlisle by the
A.6. To add to my discomfort I found that this road
was carrying a lot of heavy traffic for about 20 miles,
as the M.6 had not been opened between Carlisle and
Penrith. My target for this day was to get to the Queens
Head Hotel at Askham, a village about 4 miles south of
Penrith. I made it, but I had to rest for 15 minutes or
so when only one mile away, as I was feeling so weak.
This small hotel was quite exceptional in its decor and
furnishings, and the food, I observed, was of a high
standard. Unfortunately, although I tried, I was unable
to eat either the evening meal or breakfast. I was in a
poor state, and felt a bit worried about my condition.
However, I slept reasonably well, and was glad to have
it quiet through the hours of darkness.

Soon after 9 a.m. I was making my way through
beautiful Lowther Park, by an uphill road which, after a
mile or two, brought me back on to the A.6, which was
much quieter now. I could see the great M.6 motorway
in the valley below, and this was carrying most of the
traffic going south. At Hackthorpe, I stopped at a small
café for a few minutes, and managed to drink a cup of
coffee. The woman who served me told me that another
man with a rucksack had been in that very morning, and
he was doing a sponsored walk from Lands End to John

O'Groats and back again. I was not feeling sufficiently well to envy him!

I stopped for my lunch break in the village of Shap. Although I was glad to be able to rest for an hour or so, I was unable to eat anything, and it took a lot of will-power to get up and go on. I still had to get over the summit of Shap. I moved on at a rather slow pace up the ascending road. Although my feet had let me down, and now my inside was playing me up, my legs always felt in first-class condition, due no doubt to all the training I had done. They got me to the top, and once there I sat on a wall feeling I had had enough. I was abominably weak from lack of food. What a battle was going on! As I sat there considering the situation, a lorry came along and stopped, and the driver asked me if I wanted a lift. Contrary to all normal practice on sponsored walks, I accepted this kind offer, and was taken the 10 miles down to Kendal.

In this delightful town close to the Lake District, I was the guest of the Rev and Mrs Ronald Forward at St Thomas' Vicarage. When I told them how I was feeling, they soon got their doctor up to see me; he quickly diagnosed enteritis, and I had a temperature of 100°. His prescriptions did the trick, and the following morning I was able to eat a boiled egg and some toast. After the vicar had committed us all to the Lord, I hit the trail at about 9.30. This was Saturday and I was due to spend the week-end at the Bridge Hotel in Ingleton as I had not been able to track down any contacts in this area. During the day I managed to eat a bridge finger with a little butter and jam. I got to Ingleton at 5.50 with a sense of returning strength and health, for which I praised God. I felt I could tackle some food, and Mr Preston the hotel proprietor suggested a steak with creamed potato. I managed to eat this with some relish and with the aid of a stomach-settling potion specially mixed for me. I found out afterwards that it contained soda water and just a dash of pink gin — I felt this came under the provision of the well-known scripture, '. . . use a little wine for the sake of your stomach' (RSV).

Ingleton is famous for its caves and waterfalls, which are of exceptional beauty, and at the week-ends the place is crowded with potholers, who can easily be recognised by their special clothes and by the equipment slung over their shoulders. I should like to have visited some of the caves, but they were several miles away, and I needed to rest as much as possible. That night a riotous bunch of potholers invaded the hotel for a party which began at 9 and went on until well past midnight. They made such a shocking row that sleep was out of the question until the last of them had gone. Mr Preston apologised to me in the morning, and explained that this group had descended upon him unexpectedly, as there had been a bit of a muddle about the booking, and he didn't normally allow parties when there were residents in the hotel.

On Sunday morning I examined the hotel notice-board to find out about church services in Ingleton, and could only find details about the Church of England, so I decided to go there. On my way, however, I spotted a sign pointing to the Methodist church, and I felt constrained to join this fellowship for morning worship. It was a nice little place with a friendly atmosphere about it, and I felt at home from the start. I took the liberty of speaking to one of the deacons about my Sponsored Walk for the kingdom of God, and I told him I thought the congregation might be interested to hear briefly about it. Like most Methodist churches in the villages, this one depends on visiting preachers, and I was taken round to the vestry to meet the minister for that morning. The deacon explained about my suggestion, but the preacher feared that I might steal too much of his valuable time. I sensed how he felt and apologised for my intrusion, but suggested that if, during the service, he had a witness in his spirit that I should say a few words, then he could call on me. He did, and I was so glad to have just 5 minutes to speak about my Walk for the Lord. Several members of the congregation spoke to me afterwards and promised to pray for me. I also got an invitation out to tea.

CHAPTER ELEVEN

A church and a contact

SINCE I left Aberdeen I had stayed at eight hotels, but from now on I would be spending all my nights either with relations or with friends who had kindly offered me hospitality. I owe a great deal to all those who received me into their homes and gave me such a warm welcome, and ministered to my needs so generously.

As I left Ingleton after my week-end's rest I felt really well, and quietly confident of ultimate success. I had waked about 280 miles and was nearly half-way home. The road I had to take wended its way through delightful country for some time and then began to climb until I found myself approaching the Pennines with all their rugged grandeur. The day was dry but cloudy, with a cool breeze which made it ideal for walking. After 12 miles I reached Settle, a busy little town with some good shops and pleasant thoroughfares. As it was time for my lunch break I wondered where I should go, for it was really too cold to eat outside. I noticed the parish church nearby and thought I might find shelter there, so I tried the door and found it open. As I went in I saw a brass plate with the words, 'This pew is reserved for the verger.' It seemed right for me to slip in there for my snack. This consisted of hot tomato soup from my vacuum flask and a couple of yoghurts. As my habit is, I lifted my heart to God in thankfulness for the wonderful way He had provided for all my needs. After my light repast I dozed off for a time, and then on opening my eyes I saw a stained glass window right opposite me, depicting our Lord talking to Martha, with Mary sitting at His feet. As I reflected on the need to keep the balance in the Christian life — worship and meditation as well as witness and work — the sun broke through the clouds and shone into this lovely church, adding a special beauty to everything, especially the windows. From the outside of the church they looked frightfully drab and uninteresting; you had to be inside to appreciate their beauty and understand their meaning. So it is with the Christian life: you can only understand its meaning and glory when you are 'inside'. As I said, the sun came out, and I thought I would continue my rest outside, so I lay down among the tombstones with my rucksack for a pillow. It is quite surprising how very comfortable you can be flat on your back on the grass. As I lay there, the verger turned up to attend to one of the graves, and found this unburied body. I soon set him at his ease as I explained who I was and what sort of a hike I was doing. He seemed most interested and gladly accepted one of my booklets.

It was just after this episode that one of God's miracles of timing took place. I was leaving Settle when a car passed me, going in the opposite direction, and it sounded its horn. I took no notice, as a good many cars had been sounding their horns as they passed, having no doubt recognised me from pictures in the Press. But a few minutes later the car returned and pulled up in front of me, and a dear friend got out and greeted me. He was Campbell McAlpine, a greatly esteemed expositor of the Word of God who lives in Worthing. He has visited Eastbourne on a number of occasions. He knew nothing about my Walk, but as he passed he thought he recognised me, and had to come back to check up. We had 15 minutes together in his car, concluding with a brief time of prayer. For me, who had walked so many miles alone, this was a blessed experience. Campbell was motoring from Bradford to Grange-over-Sands, and I was walking from Aberdeen to Eastbourne, and we met just like that. Thank you Lord.

Like the eunuch I went on my way rejoicing, and without further incidents I reached Gisburn at 5.50 and was met by the Rev and Mrs Norman Maddock. They took me in their car the five miles or so to their home at Chatburn Vicarage. This was the second of my Anglican stopping places; there would be a third at Stoke-on-Trent. I also stayed with Baptists, Pentecostals, and Brethren, and enjoyed the fullest fellowship with them all. God has created a spiritual unity amongst all believers, and He surely wants us to explore to the full the richness of this oneness. Some Christians miss so much by allowing spiritual pride to keep them aloof from their brothers and sisters in Christ who, they say, 'do not belong to us'.

At the vicarage, after my usual bath and meal, I met a representative of the Press at 7 pm, and after she had gone we chatted until 10, had prayer together and then turned in. Before settling down for the night I read Psalm 41, and was especially blessed by verse 11: 'By this I know that Thou favourest me, because mine enemy doth not triumph over me.' This was far better than a sleeping pill.

CHAPTER TWELVE

The Witches Shop

AFTER a restful night I awoke to find my bedroom flooded with sunshine. This was to be my 14th walking day, and so far there had been practically no rain, and I was very grateful to God for this. Breakfast time was often a little embarrassing for me. Many of the folk with whom I stayed did not like a cooked breakfast and were content with some cereal and a piece of buttered toast, but being on a mammoth walk I was treated quite differently. I think I blushed a little when, after having my cereal, I was confronted with a plate containing several rashers of bacon (often extra thick) and a couple of fried eggs, and sometimes in addition a few sausages. Needless to say I enjoyed this lavish provision, but I did feel a little self-conscious as I noticed the frugal meal of those around me.

This 14th walking day was to be a strenuous one, although once again I was relieved of my rucksack, as my host, the Rev Norman Maddock, had business in Blackburn where I was to spend the night, and he kindly took it to my hosts there. My target was Rochdale, and arrangements had been made to pick me up from the town hall steps, take me to Blackburn for the night, and return me to Rochdale the following morning.

To get to Rochdale I had to walk a good 25 miles with some pretty stiff climbing on the way. First of all I had to take the road via Downham, which has the reputation of being one of the most beautiful villages in Britain, and from there go over the shoulder of Pendle Hill which rises to 1800 feet, and is a landmark for miles around. I climbed for about $\frac{3}{4}$ hour or so without undue fatigue, and then began a long descent to a picturesque village with the rather strange name of Place. I had been told about the Witches Shop here, and I found it, sure enough, but it appeared to be closed. However, I had a good look in the windows and I could see many odd things relating to witchcraft, which presumably could be bought. I believe this shop had some publicity recently on radio or T.V.

Seeing this shop set up a train of thought. However much we may try to smother or ignore the spiritual part of ourselves, we cannot succeed for long. As Thomas Carlyle put it in his Sartor Resartus, 'Man's unhappiness, as I construe, comes of his greatness; it is because there is an infinite in him, which, with all his cunning he can not quite bury under the Finite. Will the whole Finance Ministers and Upholsterers and Confectioners of modern Europe undertake, in joint stock Company, to make one shoeblack happy? They cannot accomplish it above an hour or two; for the shoeblack also has a soul quite other than his stomach.' It is this urge of the infinite within us that drives so many people to spiritism and the occult. They feel deep down that there is an unseen but knowable world of the spirit, and they go to dangerous extremes to find out about it. It is my deep conviction that the Bible tells us all we need to know about the 'other world', and it warns us against unhealthy curiosity. To quote but two of such passages will be sufficient: Isaiah 8.19 (RSV), 'And when they say to you, "Consult the mediums and the wizards who chirp and mutter," should not a people consult their God?' Leviticus 20.6 (RSV), "If a person turns to mediums and wizards, playing the harlot after them, I will set my face against that person, and will cut him off from among his people."

By the middle of the day I reached Burnley, and as I entered this sizeable town I sensed an air of sadness about the place. Perhaps this had been caused by the relegation of the famous Burnley football team into the Second Division, after more than 50 years in the First; or perhaps it was just my imagination.

I was feeling hungry and I had by this time worked off my V.I.P. breakfast, so I slipped into a tiny fish and chip shop, attracted there by the appetising smell that always seems to hang around such places. A stout but very active woman was handing out portions of fish and chips to a queue of folk, but, when my turn came, I asked for mine to be served in the little dining-room at the back of the shop. Before I had taken my seat at the table, there was my plateful of good, nourishing food and a nice cup of tea to go with it — and this for just a few new pence.

I made my way through the rest of the town, and on the outskirts I discovered a lovely little park, adjoining the golf course, and here I had my '40 winks' plus. When I resumed I found that my road led uphill for several miles until it reached a sort of plateau, and this continued for a few more miles until the road descended to Bacup; I had another eight miles to go to reach Rochdale. I got there at 5.30 and made my way to the town hall, where I was picked up by some kind friends and taken off to Blackburn, a distance of about 18 miles. My link with Blackburn goes back to 1917 when as a boy of 12 I first met Peter Sharratt. He was convalescing in Eastbourne from the effects of mustard gas received in France during the First World War, and his home was in Blackburn. Some missionary relations of our family were known to the Sharratts, and this proved to be the link which brought us together. Uncle Peter was used by God to be a great blessing to me and my brothers and sister, and we often spent some of our school holidays in the Sharratt home. Uncle Peter went home to glory last year and it was my great privilege to assist at the funeral service. His two sisters continue to live in the old home, and this is where I spent the night.

Before turning in, our conversation dwelt on many things including the need for the Holy Spirit to be released in us, especially when we meet for worship. It so often happens that when Christians gather for this purpose they seem to be possessed by a spirit of gloom and cold religion. We need to break through into spontaneous praise, but to be real we need above everything else the power and liberty of the Holy Spirit.

CHAPTER THIRTEEN

The big cities

I WAS taken back to Rochdale by a kind osteopath, who, in spite of the fact that he had an appointment in Blackburn soon after 9 am, found time to cover the 36 miles to Rochdale and back so as to put me down at my starting place. This was quite a different day, as most of it seemed to be spent in walking through Manchester, one of our largest cities. I found this rather depressing because of the tremendous number of shops and houses which had been pulled down, particularly in the suburbs, and no attempt had been made to tidy up, and there were no signs of any re-building programme. I noticed the same thing in Burnley and later on in Birmingham. The reason could have been lack of money, or perhaps the failure to decide what to do with these derelict sites. In spite of its size I did not find Manchester difficult to get through. I found my way fairly easily to Piccadilly and had my snack in the Piccadilly Gardens, which were crowded when I got there about 1 o'clock. I found a deck-chair and settled down to eat my soft rolls spread with butter and red currant jelly, and then a yoghurt and a drink from my flask.

I left Manchester by the A.34, a road that was going to dominate a lot of my walking for some time. It was a pleasant road with a footpath for a good many miles, as I was walking through built-up areas. I had left the peaceful countryside behind and until I got south of Birmingham I would be in sight of cities and chimneys and factories. The A.34 took me all the way to Handforth where I was to spend the night. I found the house where I was to stay without difficulty as I had been given a sketch map to guide me. This was a most comfortable home in which, amongst other things, there was colour T.V. After a bath and a meal I watched 'It's a Knockout' and marvelled at the ingenuity of those who plan these competitions.

The Rev P. L. C. Smith of Burslem Rectory, who was to be my next host, phoned through to say that if I arrived in time the Stoke radio might want to interview me at the studios. Mr Conn, a member of the Board of the Hour of Revival, also phoned to say that at the Board meeting held in London that day he had been asked to convey the good wishes of the Board to me. I so enjoyed relaxing in the super, reclining, leather-upholstered chairs that I went to bed rather late, feeling pleasantly tired.

I awoke to another fine day, and after a good breakfast I thanked my kind hosts and made my way back to the A.34. Before leaving Eastbourne I had not realised the advantage of walking north to south rather than in the opposite direction. As I walked southwards I always had the sun in front of me — much more pleasant than having the sun on one's back. There is a simple lesson to be learned from this, which someone has expressed thus: 'Turn your face to the sun and you will find that all the shadows fall behind.' Faber put the same truth in another way:

> If our love were but more simple
> We should take Him at His word;
> And our lives would be all sunshine
> In the sweetness of our Lord.

I reached Congleton in good time, and, as I was leaving it, the Rev and Mrs Smith found me and kindly offered to take my rucksack the remaining 10 miles or so. Before they left me I checked my route and the way to their home on a small sketch map they had kindly drawn for me and sent to me before I left Eastbourne. In spite of this I went wrong at a roundabout in Chell and added about three miles to my day's walk which must have been about 28 miles. I did not get to the rectory, where I was to stay, until after 6.30. It was then too late to go to the B.B.C. studios, but I was contacted on the road the following day. The Smiths have two children, and I was particularly interested in their son who was at a sixth form college in Stoke. I believe there are a few of these colleges in the country, started by way of an experiment, and from what I was able to glean they are proving to be a real success. Mrs Smith kindly did a little washing for me and got it all nicely dried by the morning.

It was Friday May 21st, my 17th walking day; glorious sunshine again. How blessed I had been in the weather! How different things might have been if I had had to contend with heavy rain, but so far it had been ideal walking weather. Soon after starting I was tracked down by a representative of the B.B.C. who invited me into his car for a recorded interview, which he said would be heard on the Stoke radio at 12.50 pm that day. Amongst other things he asked me what I thought about all day and what I did as I walked all alone. I told him that I frequently sang praises to the Lord and talked to Him as I walked along. I also told him of the contacts I often had with people, and I handed him one of the booklets which I invariably use. I should like to have heard all this over the radio, but of course I was probably fast asleep in a field at the time of the broadcast. During the day I was also able to have a word with a man in a shop and with two labourers who were digging a hole in the road.

After my lunch break I got up, slung my rucksack on my back, and went on through Stafford, and after a few more miles I came to Penkridge. It had been arranged for Mr Davies, the Accountant of the Hour of Revival Association, to pick me up here and take me to his home at Shifnal about 15 miles away. I phoned him from a garage and he came out to meet me, but there was a little misunderstanding about which garage I was waiting at, and this delayed our meeting for an extra half hour or so. Mr and Mrs Davies have a delightful house adjoining a farm and I so enjoyed being away from the noise of traffic, and from the sight of factories and their tall chimneys, and to be deep in the country once again. Mr Davies has his own geese, and when I was there the parents were strutting about with five goslings; a pretty sight. There was also a lovely old Labrador, a cat and some hens. The adjoining farm had a large number of cows, and when I got up the next morning they were all gathered beneath my bedroom window. As usual I slept well and there was nothing to disturb me save the occasional hooting of an owl.

Saturday May 22nd. Mr Davies kindly offered to take my rucksack to my daughter Rosalyn's flat in Selly Oak, Birmingham, so that I might be free of it for the day. Before doing this he took me back to Penkridge where I had to start my walk. The Press had wanted to see me here at 9.30, but I let them know that I must be away by 9 am, and suggested that they look for me on the road between Penkridge and Cannock. They found me all right, and we had a few minutes together when they asked me questions about my Walk and took photographs; as usual, I gave them booklets. After 3½ hours' walking I found an attractive park a few miles short of Walsall and stopped there for my snack and rest. I left at 1.30 and walked until 6.15 with only one short stop of 15 minutes or so. It took me those 4½ hours to get to Selly Oak. I found Birmingham a very difficult place to walk through. I entered it from the north and had to walk right through the centre, and a further three miles from the Bull Ring to my daughter's flat. I had quite a bit of trouble with the huge pedestrian subways, when I had to go down and then up again. Frequently I came up the wrong exit and felt rather like a rabbit running up and down holes in the ground. It was no doubt good exercise, but when you have been walking all day it's not very funny.

Rosalyn gave me a loving welcome and said she was surprised to see me looking so well. I *was* feeling fit. The Lord's Name be praised! Andrew Ramsey, my son-in-law, was away in Gravesend visiting his parents when I arrived, but he returned on Sunday evening. The Ramseys have a nice little flat just off the Bristol road, over a doctor's surgery, and immediately opposite is the Pentecostal church which they attend. One of their rooms they call the Unusual Room, and here they have an old horn-type gramophone which works, a large Union Jack for a curtain, a framed newspaper-cutting showing Adolf Hitler in 1937, and a variety of carpet squares sewn together to make the carpet.

I had been asked by Pastor Alan Caple to speak at the morning service on my experiences since leaving Aberdeen. There were about 250 present and there was a wonderful spirit of worship and praise, and the singing was a real inspiration. It was easy to talk in that atmosphere and I felt very happy in doing this bit of service for the Lord. I was also given a few minutes to speak at the evening service when there must have been over 300 present. This is a really live church with lots of young people and frequent conversions. The Christian fellowship was truly wonderful and a real inspiration and uplift.

Rosalyn produced an excellent lunch of pork chops with all the trimmings, followed by fruit salad and ice-cream, but she also went to church. Some housewives say that they cannot cook a Sunday dinner and also go to church. To use a common expression, this is all bunkum. For many years we, as a family, have always gone to church together on a Sunday morning and then come home to an appetising lunch of roast lamb or pork, with the other things like roast potatoes and green peas; followed by apple or plum pie. My wife placed this all in the oven (with the exception of the peas) before leaving for church. Of course this does mean having breakfast at a reasonable time. Rosalyn had learned the art of doing this from a very efficient mother.

I rested in the afternoon while my daughter took a Sunday school class, then we had tea together and soon afterwards we went across the road to the Elim church, for the evening service. And so a very happy day ended and I went to bed refreshed in spirit, soul, and body.

CHAPTER FOURTEEN

Pork pies and wigs

THE light rain which had fallen yesterday had died out and, as I prepared to set out on my last full week, the sun was shining and it seemed very warm. To enable me to get to the A.34 without going back into the centre of Birmingham, Andrew had worked out a suitable route which took me in a south easterly direction, and without any difficulty I found my way to the road I wanted, which was to take me to Stratford-on-Avon. This turned out to be the warmest day I had had so far, and some of the delightful places I passed through, like Henley-in-Arden, looked their best in the bright sunshine.

Although the day was hot I did not find it oppressive, and I managed to maintain my average of 3½ mph. I got to Stratford at about 6 o'clock. I doubt if anyone can enter this place without thinking of the mighty genius who was born there; I refer, of course, to William Shakespeare. Many great phrases and sentences from his plays have become part of our English language, and some words from a speech put into the mouth of Brutus towards the end of Julius Caesar have been with me for some days:

There is a tide in the affairs of men,
Which, taken at the flood, leads on to fortune;
Omitted, all the voyage of their life
Is bound in shallows and in miseries.
On such a full sea are we now afloat,
And we must take the current when it serves,
Or lose our ventures.

I have often thought of that day in October when the challenge to do this Sponsored Walk came to me. I am so glad that I did not refuse and miss the opportunity of a lifetime to do something rather special. It might never have come again. These words of Shakespeare mean quite simply that when the opportunity to do some big thing comes we should grasp it with both hands or run the risk of 'losing our ventures'.

Having got to Stratford I then set about finding my host for the night. I had been told that he lived in a flat over Mitchells the bakers in Wood Street, so after seeking directions from one or two passers-by I found my way to the shop. I rang the bell and Paul Plank answered it. He was about 25 years of age and, as I discovered later, a bachelor. He runs the bakery business and lives in the flat by himself. His parents live in Stratford-on-Avon, but as Paul has to be down in the bakery by 4 am he prefers to live as close to his job as possible. This was the only time I was entertained by a bachelor, and I could not help wondering how he managed. My first impressions were favourable when he produced a nice pot of tea and some cakes immediately I arrived. I learned a little about his business as we chatted together over our cups of tea. Although the baking of bread occupied the early hours of the day, followed by the making of doughnuts, the main job is done in the afternoon which is entirely given up to the production of pork pies, thousands of them.

Paul suggested that I had a bath and rested for a short time while he prepared the evening meal. I wondered what he would produce. Would it be pork pies? Later we sat down together in a small kitchen which was well equipped, and from the hot oven Paul brought out two large plates on each of which there was an enormous helping — pork chops, cauliflower, carrots, potatoes, and apple sauce. I have a pretty good appetite and on my Walk I could cope with anything set before me, but I must confess that Paul's provision beat me and I had to leave a little. The meal was rounded up with a liberal helping of fruit salad and thick cream.

As this had been such a hot day I decided to lighten my rucksack by sending several things home, including my thick windcheater, which had been a good standby in the colder days.

I did not hear Paul get up for his early start in the bakery, but I did hear him come back about 7.30 to get breakfast. Before retiring for the night Paul pointed out there was a 'Teasmade' in my bedroom, and he had set it for 7 a.m. I awoke to hear the water in the kettle boiling its head off, but for some reason or other, unknown to me, none of this boiling water seemed to have the slightest inclination of going into the teapot. There must have been a mechanical defect that morning, so I was done out of my nice cup of tea. I did not miss it much as this is one of life's luxuries that I don't indulge in when at home.

Soon after Paul got back he set about getting the breakfast, and it wasn't long before I heard the lovely sizzling sound of bacon and eggs cooking. This typically English breakfast makes a good start to any day, and I felt well fed and ready for another 25 miles or so. Then Paul went back to his bread, doughnuts, and pork pies, and I hit the trail once again. From one of the warmest days this turned out to be one of my coldest, and I began to wonder if I had been wise in sending my windcheater home. It is sometimes said that in Britain we don't have a climate, we just have weather. Perhaps one of the factors that has toughened us as a nation has been this great variety in our weather which can produce almost anything within the space of 24 hours.

This turned out to be a good day for witnessing. Near Shipston-on-Stour two nice young fellows in a car, returning from a job they had been on in Oxford, stopped and told me that they had seen me earlier in the day, and they wanted to know what I was doing. This gave me the chance to tell them about my Sponsored Walk and why I was doing it, and to add a few words about the Lord Jesus and then give them booklets. Soon after this, because the day was rather cool, I went into a café for my mid-day snack, and while there I was able to say a few words for the Lord and pass on a booklet or two.

In mid-afternoon when I was climbing the long hill from Long Compton towards Chipping Norton a man of about 35 pulled up in his car and offered me a lift. I thanked him for his kindness and then explained that as I was on a sponsored walk I could not accept his kind offer. After I had told him what I was doing he said he was interested in 'that sort of thing' and handed me a £1 note. Forty minutes later (he had apparently been to get a coffee in Long Compton) he overtook me again and stopped for a few more words. I prayed for his salvation.

By late afternoon I was approaching Chipping Norton which is just a mile or so off the A.34. I had arranged to meet Mr Mulley of Banbury in the lounge of the White Hart Hotel at 6 pm, but I got there at 5 pm and I wondered if I ought to phone him and let him know of my early arrival. On second thoughts I decided not to interfere with the arrangements already made. I went into the hotel and ordered a pot of tea and biscuits, changed into my long trousers, and after a wash settled down to enjoy my 'cuppa' and write up my diary. At 6 pm exactly Mr Mulley arrived and took me in his car to his lovely home on the outskirts of Banbury. Mr and Mrs Mulley have a fine old house, spacious and dignified, with beautiful gardens, and lawns graced by flowers and trees in great variety. What used to be the coach houses have been converted into a wig factory, where some 70 people are employed. I understand that Mulleys of Banbury are one of the largest wig-makers in England. I was introduced to several members of the staff who had sponsored me, and I was able to have a brief peep inside the factory. Most of the staff come from the surrounding villages, and they are glad to be able to work in such delightful surroundings. I should like to have learned a bit more about the making of wigs, but there really was not time.

The Mulleys treated me with the greatest kindness and I very much enjoyed my short stay with them. After breakfast the Bibles were brought out and we read the Scripture Union portion for the day. I felt very much at home doing this, as my wife and I make it our practice to read the Scriptures after breakfast every morning, and we have done this ever since our wedding day in 1940. As our children grew up and learned to read, they took their turn in assisting at our morning devotions. They

are all grown up now; our eldest is 29 and our youngest
is 18, and they all (five of them) love the Lord Jesus and
are happily engaged in His service. I feel sure that the
habit of daily Bible reading in our home through the
years has had a great deal to do with the blessing which
we have seen in our family.

The Scripture Union portion read that morning at the
Mulleys breakfast table was 3 John 1-8 (RSV), part of
which reads as follows: 'Beloved, it is a loyal thing you
do when you render any service to the brethren, especially
to strangers . . . You will do well to send them on their
journey as befits God's service.' The Daily Bread notes
which we also read include the following comment: 'John
is referring to the very important practice in those days
of looking after Christians who were travelling from place
to place. This kindness was appreciated because distances
were long and travelling very slow.' The commentator
adds a paragraph which I can truly make my own: 'I
have been a traveller and have stayed in countless homes,
small and great, rich and poor. I cannot be sufficiently
grateful for the kindness and care I have received. If any
of my hostesses read this, thank you. Do remember that
if you can do nothing else for Christ, this is a 'loyal thing'
and a greatly appreciated service.'

CHAPTER FIFTEEN

Old Father Thames

MR MULLEY took me back to my starting point and I got going at about 9.30 and walked for three hours and then stopped at the Marlborough Inn, two miles north of Woodstock, for a Scotch egg salad and coffee. I was able to give the proprietor of the inn one of my booklets. Woodstock, of course, is famous because Blenheim Palace is there. I caught a glimpse of it at the end of the long avenue of trees and thought of the man who was born there, and who has been described as 'The Greatest Englishman'. I wish I could have spared the time to visit this Palace, but my schedule was pretty tight and I had to go on with my Walk.

I reached north Oxford in good time and was soon able to find the home where I was to spend the night.

I left Oxford by the Magdalen Bridge. The Press had asked me to meet them there for some photographs. For the first time since I left Aberdeen it was pouring with rain, and the bridge presented a dismal scene as crowds of folk crossed it on their way to work, and hundreds of cars splashed their way into the city. I was glad of my waterproof Cagoule which covered most of me, and I set out against the stream of traffic for my next 'port of call' which was Henley-on-Thames. To get away from the constant stream of traffic I took a minor road to Sandford-on-Thames, but unfortunately, after passing through this place and rejoining the dual carriage-way. I went off in the wrong direction. I didn't discover my error until I had walked 1½ miles, thus adding 3 miles to my already long day. Walking on the dual carriage-way was most unpleasant as there was no footpath and I was constantly being splashed by the cars and lorries as they went by. I got uncomfortably wet.

My son Jonathan had written telling me that he would be motoring in the Oxford area on this day and he would

be looking out for me. By 12.30 the weather had improved
a little and I was approaching Dorchester where I thought
I might have my break and get a spot of lunch, and pos-
sibly a 'dry-out'. I was sorry not to have seen anything
of my son, and could only assume we had missed each
other. I noticed an inn which looked a likely place and
went in and ordered some food. Unfortunately there were
no drying facilities available, so I had to content myself
with a change of socks. After my snack I put my feet up
and dozed off for a while, and, after a half hour or so,
in my sleepy state I heard people entering the dining-room.
I slowly opened one eye and there sitting in the chair
beside me was my grand-daughter Vivienne. My son,
with his wife and two children, Vivienne age 3 and
Timothy 10 months, had tracked me down, rather cleverly
I thought, and we had quite a re-union. Jonathan paid for
my lunch.

By the time I got going again the rain had stopped
and the clouds had lifted and were breaking up. It wasn't
long before the sun came out and my sopping wet shoes
began to dry out. From Oxford to Henley is a good 25
miles, and with the three extra miles I had given myself
this was a pretty strenuous day. However, I now had a
footpath to go on and the weather was good, so I felt
cheerful — and grateful. When I was a few miles short
of Henley I was feeling very thirsty and, as I had nothing
with me to slake my thirst, I looked around for the answer
to my need. I spotted a couple of cottages not far away
and at one of them two women were having a chin-wag,
so I asked if I might have my flask filled with water. This
they readily did, and I went away a short distance, and
sat down on a grassy bank to have my drink, when one
of the women came after me with a nice cup of coffee
which I drank with relish. I was able to say a few words
and hand her one of my booklets.

The approach to Henley is very beautiful and although I was feeling a bit tired I enjoyed those last few
miles. I got to Henley at 6.30 pm but I still had to find
my way to the home of Mr and Mrs Spraggs, who had
kindly supplied me with a small sketch map. I found

that I had another two miles to do and that was mostly uphill, so by the time I reached my destination I had walked 30 miles. Mr and Mrs Spraggs seemed really concerned about me as they had expected me to arrive on Monday and this was Thursday. The reason for this muddle was that when I wrote to my hosts at Stratford-on-Avon and Henley, advising them of my week's delay, I put the letters in the wrong envelopes. For the first time my lines of communication had got crossed. I am afraid I must have put my hosts to some additional trouble owing to this misunderstanding, but they treated me well, and we enjoyed good fellowship.

The shoes I had been wearing were badly in need of attention and after breakfast Mr Spraggs took me to a shoe repairer in Henley to see if he could do a quick job for me. He was unable to, but suggested that I called at their other shop in Twyford, about five miles away. I said goodbye to my kind friends, and then crossed the bridge over the River Thames. What a lovely spot this is, with the wide, flowing river, and numerous boats of many shapes and sizes moored to the banks. I walked on the road to Wargrave and caught frequent glimpses of the river, and I rather envied those who owned boathouses and private yachts or motor-launches. Before very long I reached Twyford, and called at the shoe shop to see if anything could be done to my shoes. They seemed to be expecting me, and I found that they had had a phone call from Henley about me. I took off my shoes and waited in the shop while they did the necessary repairs. Within half an hour they handed my shoes back to me, soled and heeled, and they refused to make any charge. Another token of the Lord's goodness to me. We do well to recognise the kindness of the Lord in the small things of life. We know from the Bible that God is interested in what we eat, and what we wear, and in all things which concern us. He can help even in getting a pair of shoes mended. How much happier our lives would be if we made it our practice to consult the Lord about everything!

CHAPTER SIXTEEN

The last stages

THIS was Friday and I was greatly looking forward to my final week-end which I was to spend with my brother in Camberley. He lives with his wife and son in a delightful house in this lovely Surrey town. When I was about six miles away, my brother found me and kindly took my rucksack. He returned home in his car and then walked out to meet me so that he could conduct me for the last two miles or so. We met near the Sandhurst Military Academy and made our way through the beautiful grounds, which were looking their best on this late spring day.

My original plan was to spend the Friday with my relations, and go on to friends at Godalming for the week-end, but owing to my change of date they could not have me. My alternative plan was to walk in the general direction of Horsham on the Saturday and get my brother to pick me up from point X and return me there on Monday morning; he kindly agreed to fit in with these arrangements. To save me walking on major roads he worked out a route using B roads and going through lovely scenery, including the Hog's Back and the picturesque village of Compton. On this Saturday I was able to enjoy another of God's timing miracles. In the middle of the afternoon as I emerged from the last of the minor roads to join the main Guildford-Horsham road I noticed a footpath on the opposite side, but before I could cross I had to wait to allow several cars to pass. One of these slowed down and pulled into the side of the road, and there was my son Jonathan and his wife and family. They were returning to Eastbourne from Swindon, and at the exact moment when I came out of the small road they came by and spotted me. Had I been 30 seconds later we should not have met. I was reminded of the words of the Psalmist, 'My times are in Thy hands', and so it was in this case.

After this happy interlude I walked on for another 1½ hours or so, when I was about 12 miles short of Horsham; then I phoned my brother at Camberley, told him where I was, and sat down with my back against a tree and waited. Although I had walked some 20 miles it didn't seem long before my brother arrived in his car to take me back to Camberley. We spent most of the evening chatting and sharing our family news, in which Paul my nephew joined. We turned in at 10.30.

I was near enough to the end of my Walk to think about drafting a letter to be sent out to all my sponsors, giving them a short account of my adventures, and ask-ing for the money which had been promised. I spent some of Sunday doing this, but in the morning I went to the Camberley Parish Church and joined in worship with a good company. Before entering the church a small, cherubic choir-boy pointed what looked like a gun at me, and ran off laughing. This being Whit-Sunday, the visiting preacher gave us a thoughtful message on the power of the Holy Spirit seen in the lives of the early disciples. He emphasised the fact that their experience could be ours today. How much of our Christian service is 'beating the air'; how we need the manifestation of the power of God in our work for Him, and for daily living. The early believers lived in the abiding sense of the presence of Christ, made possible by the indwelling Holy Spirit, and this experience can be ours today in the same measure.

My sister-in-law is an excellent cook and she provided a special lunch to celebrate the successful completion of my Walk, which was imminent. Amongst other things we had Angus roast beef, the beef having been obtained from a butcher some miles away who specialises in this luxury. A restful afternoon came to an end with the partaking of tea in my brother's caravan which was parked at the end of his garden. The week-end passed all too quickly, but I was quite eager to get started on my last three days; I was due back in Eastbourne on Wednesday.

Monday morning was beautiful with brilliant sunshine and the birds singing their joyful songs. I was feeling fit

and ready to be off. In my devotions I read, '. . . foras-
much as ye know that your labour is not in vain in the
Lord.' Thanks be unto God who giveth us the victory.
How very near this was for me! Joan made me up a nice
lunch which included a hard-boiled egg, some crisp bread
and a yoghurt. My brother took me back to point X,
about 12 miles from Horsham, and I soon got into my
stride again, and after tramping some 13 miles, which
took me past Horsham, I stopped for lunch. When I
resumed I had about 11 miles to go to Haywards Heath
where I was to spend the night with Mr John Payne, the
manager of the main branch of Barclays Bank, and an
old colleague of mine. About 8 miles from Haywards
Heath I got a cup of coffee from a machine outside a
hotel which was closed, and as I was enjoying this a
friend who lives at Hampden Park near Eastbourne found
me. He had been given my probable route on this day.
For many years he had been crippled by arthritis and
could only walk with the aid of two sticks, but as a result of operations on both his hips he could walk almost
normally. He insisted on walking about $\frac{1}{2}$ mile with me
before he was picked up by car. It was truly wonderful
to see him almost skipping along.

I was able to give away three booklets that day — two
in a shop and one to a girl who kindly filled my flask with
a lemon drink. She lived in the charming village of War-
linglid not far from Haywards Heath.

I found the Paynes' house without difficulty, in fact,
Mr Payne and one of his sons was out looking for me.
It was good to renew fellowship with John again. I was
his second-in-command when he was manager of one of
the Eastbourne branches of the bank. We talked over
the many changes that have taken place in the banking
world during the past few years, and as I have two sons
in Barclays Bank I was fairly *au fait* with what has been
happening. It was a delight to spend a few hours in this
Christian home, and as this was Whit-Monday I was especially grateful to the Paynes for receiving me so warmly
into their family circle.

The sun was shining when I awoke, and I praised the

Lord for His greatness and His goodness. 'He is greatly
to be praised from the rising of the sun until the going
down of the same.' We rob God when we do not praise
Him. As I only had 13 miles to go I was able to enjoy
a leisurely breakfast with Mr and Mrs Payne and their
three delightful children. The Press had asked to see me
at 9 o'clock so John went down to his office to take a
look at the post, and then came back so as to be present
at this interview, and to bid me farewell.

Before leaving Haywards Heath I bought one or two
things for my picnic lunch, including some sausage rolls;
it was the first time I had indulged in sausage rolls, but
somehow I fancied them on this day. I took the Scaynes
Hill road and passed many attractive houses on the way.
Being only 30 miles from London, Haywards Heath is
well within the commuter belt and house property is in
great and constant demand, and as a consequence prices
are high. The surrounding countryside is as beautiful as
any in Sussex, and this adds to the attraction of this
town. From Scaynes Hill I went on to Chailey, and near
here I was overtaken by the Press who wanted to get
some photographs; but before they got down to work
they handed me a choc-ice. How very thoughtful! I was
soon able to turn off the main road and get on to a minor
road signposted 'Barcombe', and from there I went
through Barcombe Mills. After joining the A.26 for a
few hundred yards I turned into the Ringmer road and
reached this quiet and peaceful Sussex village in mid-
afternoon. Mrs Rice, the widow of Dr Rice who was a
well-known figure in Ringmer, had kindly offered me
hospitality, but when I arrived rather earlier than expected she was at a womens meeting in connection with the
church, but her son Christopher was there to welcome
me. Christopher is about 20, and when I saw him all
kinds of memories were stirred in me. When he was at
school in Eastbourne, first at Nevill House Preparatory
School and later at Eastbourne College, he used to stay
with us during the week and return to Ringmer at the
week-ends. He shared a large bedroom with one of my
sons, who was at the same prep school, and what rowdy

times they had in that 'dormitory'! I sometimes have nostalgic feelings when I think of those days when our family were all young and we had such rollicking times together. These feelings don't last long, but are soon replaced by a sense of wonder at the goodness of God who has kept us so close to one another through the years and up to the present time.

I left home on 24th April and I had therefore been away just over five weeks, and I knew that a great welcome awaited me in Eastbourne on the following day. I was due at the Upperton Road end of Enys Road at 3 pm. My wife and family felt they would like to anticipate this, so they came over to Ringmer at about 9 pm and we had a very happy re-union. They seemed a little surprised to see me looking so well and slim; I had lost a stone during my long Walk. We shared our news over coffee and they left about 10.30; I turned in and slept like a log.

CHAPTER SEVENTEEN
The end of the journey

MY waking thoughts were directed to the Lord, who had brought me through many and varied experiences, and who had been with me over the many miles. He had enabled me to complete the task to which I believe I was called. I had never really doubted that I should win through, and even when I was being tested I had a quiet confidence that all would be well. I know that I was surrounded and upheld by the prayers of many of God's children every day, and this enabled me to 'walk and not faint'.

Caroline my younger daughter wanted to walk with me on my last day, and so her brother Nicolas, who works at Lewes, brought her out to meet me. We linked up at Glyndebourne and I was glad to have company on the last 14 miles. Mr Eric Redfern, the Editor of the Eastbourne Gazette and Eastbourne Herald, had instructed a reporter and a photographer to shadow me for the final 12 miles. Pictures were taken at all the signposts on the route, and the reporter was able to get some final facts from me for his paper. We all stopped at Wilmington for coffee.

We reached Polegate — 4 miles from Eastbourne — at 12.30 and, as arranged, my wife was there to meet us with a picnic lunch which we enjoyed at the recreation ground. At 1.30 Carol and I set off at a leisurely pace, for we were not expected in Eastbourne until 3 pm. I had heard about the many plans which had been made to welcome me, and I must confess to some excitement at the prospect of reaching the 'finishing tape'. When I got there just a few minutes before 3 o'clock, there was a crowd of about 100 waiting for me. Some were carrying banners with suitable wording such as, 'Welcome home, Willie', 'Aberdeen to Eastbourne : Well walked, Willie', '570 Miles pilgrimage for Christ'. There were also several cars with bunting and suitable texts displayed. It all presented a very happy scene, and I felt greatly honoured.

Amongst the first to greet me were Dr and Mrs Eric Hutchings who had done so much to make the Walk such a success.

After many handshakes and greetings we all moved off in the direction of the Hour of Revival studios, feeling very important with our police escort. As the procession moved along Terminus Road, Eastbourne's main thoroughfare, people waved from the windows of buildings, and many on the streets greeted me as I passed by.

The Mayor of Eastbourne, Councillor John Robinson, was waiting at the studios to give me an official welcome, and I was deeply moved by the warmth and sincerity of his greeting. When as many as possible had crowded in, the Mayor said a few more appropriate words; Dr Hutchings followed, and then I gave a brief account of my experiences on my long journey. Tea followed, and I was able to walk amongst my many friends and thank them personally for their interest in me during my absence. It was a great finish to an exciting undertaking.

I was reminded of that well-known prayer of Sir Francis Drake, 'O Lord God, when Thou givest Thy servants to endeavour any great matter, grant us also to know that it is not the beginning but the continuing of the same until it is thoroughly finished which yieldeth the true glory; through Him, who, for the finishing of Thy work, laid down His life, our Redeemer Jesus Christ.'